BONYO BONYO

The True Story of a Brave Boy from Kenya

OCEAN

AFRICA

KENYA

Vanita's Dedication

This book is dedicated to Bonyo Bonyo and millions of others like him whose dreams brought them to America with the promise they might be fulfilled.

It is also dedicated to all of my grandchildren in the hope that their dreams are as big as Bonyo Bonyo's and that, like him, they will help others as they, too, were helped.

Acknowledgments

Mike Blanc
Kristin Blackwood
Dr. Bonyo Bonyo
Mrs. Sharon Leonard
Dr. Ellen Kempf
Dr. Jeff Kempf
Kurt Landefeld
Paul Royer
Jennie Levy Smith
Sheila Tarr
Elaine Mesek
Michael Olin-Hitt
David Shoenfelt
Carolyn Brodie
Gailmarie Fort

Bonyo Bonyo
The True Story of a Brave Boy from Kenya
VanitaBooks, LLC
All rights reserved.
Copyright © 2010 Vanita Oelschlager

Text by Vanita Oelschlager
Illustrations by Kristin Blackwood and Mike Blanc

Printed in China.
Hardcover Edition ISBN 978-0-9819714-3-8
Paperback Edition ISBN 978-0-9819714-4-5

www.VanitaBooks.com

BONYO BONYO

The True Story of a Brave Boy from Kenya

by Vanita Oelschlager

Illustrations by
Kristin Blackwood and Mike Blanc

VanitaBooks, LLC

This is a true story.

It is about a brave boy from Kenya.

Kenya is a country on the continent of Africa.

This boy grew up to become a doctor.

This is the story of Bonyo Bonyo

as he told it to me.

"My name is Bonyo Bonyo. My first name is the same as my last name which may seem funny in the United States, but in Kenya, this is normal.

"I think I was born in September of 1962, but I am not sure. We didn't celebrate birthdays and not much about us was written down.

"I grew up in Western Kenya, near Kisumu. There were five in my family, and we were farmers.

"We ate mostly 'ugali.' This is a kind of meal ground from corn. You would call it corn meal or corn bread. We were poor and sometimes hungry. But my father and mother worked hard. And we learned to work hard too. We ate the food we grew on our farm. We had brown cows and goats, too.

"I had fun when I was growing up. We played soccer. We had no soccer ball so we made one out of cloth that we sewed together. Then we stuffed it with whatever we could find.

"I also loved to listen to stories told by my granny. She told us stories while smoking a long pipe. She told us stories of warriors, traditional dances and weddings.

"She would also tell horror stories about jaguars, lions and hyenas. When I got older I thought Granny told us those stories so she could go to sleep at night and not worry about us going out in the dark.

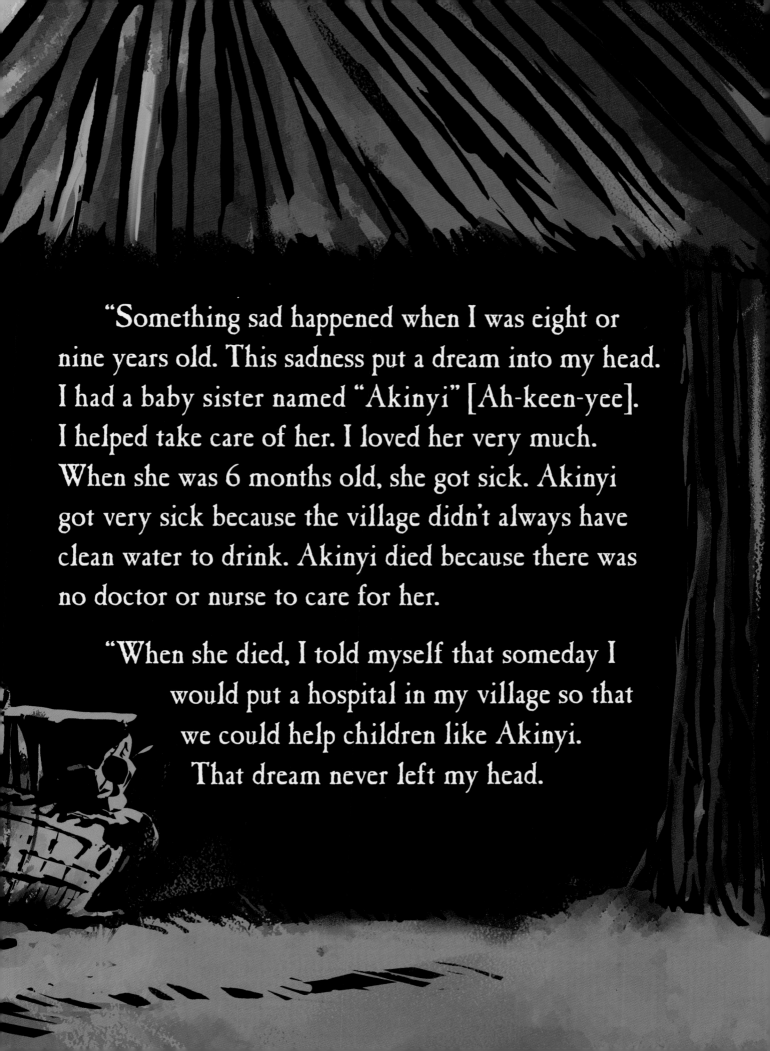

"Something sad happened when I was eight or nine years old. This sadness put a dream into my head. I had a baby sister named "Akinyi" [Ah-keen-yee]. I helped take care of her. I loved her very much. When she was 6 months old, she got sick. Akinyi got very sick because the village didn't always have clean water to drink. Akinyi died because there was no doctor or nurse to care for her.

"When she died, I told myself that someday I would put a hospital in my village so that we could help children like Akinyi. That dream never left my head.

"School was important in my village. I knew if I was going to help my village, I needed to go to school. I walked 90 minutes each day to get to school. School cost one dollar a year. When I was to go into 7th grade, my parents didn't have the dollar to send me that year.

"Since I couldn't go to school, I helped my mother. One day she sent me to the shop in the village. The shop was like a general store where you could get sugar, salt and other things for cooking. I rode there on a bike that was too big for me. I rode under the bar on the bike.

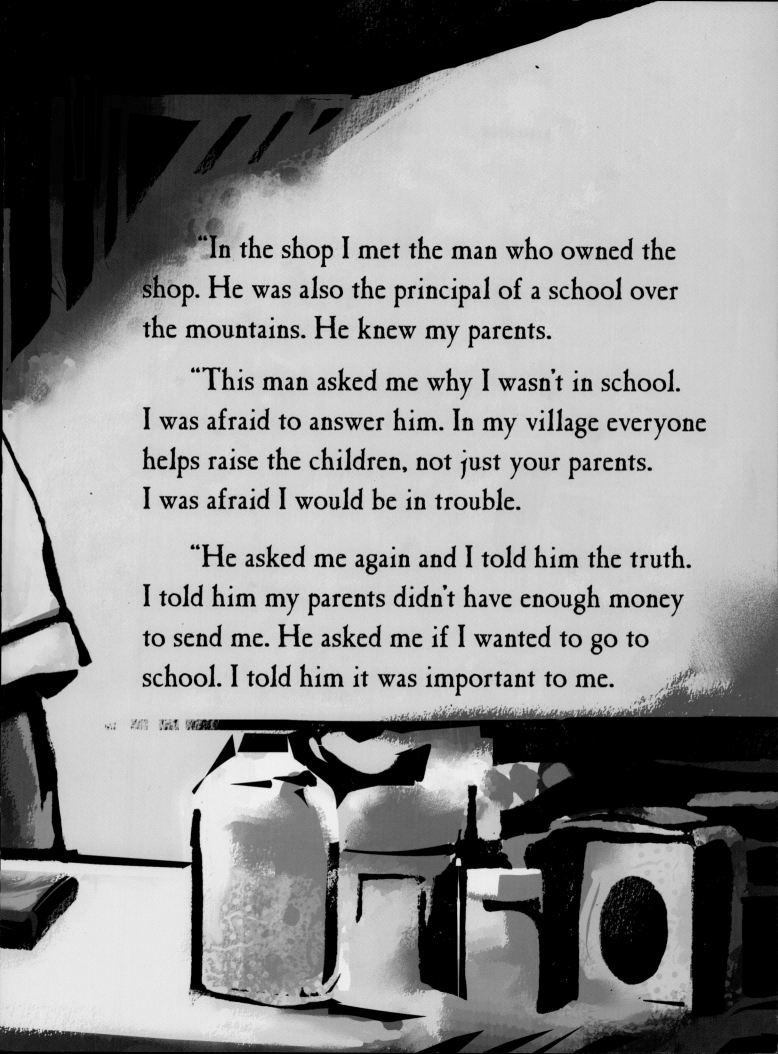

"In the shop I met the man who owned the shop. He was also the principal of a school over the mountains. He knew my parents.

"This man asked me why I wasn't in school. I was afraid to answer him. In my village everyone helps raise the children, not just your parents. I was afraid I would be in trouble.

"He asked me again and I told him the truth. I told him my parents didn't have enough money to send me. He asked me if I wanted to go to school. I told him it was important to me.

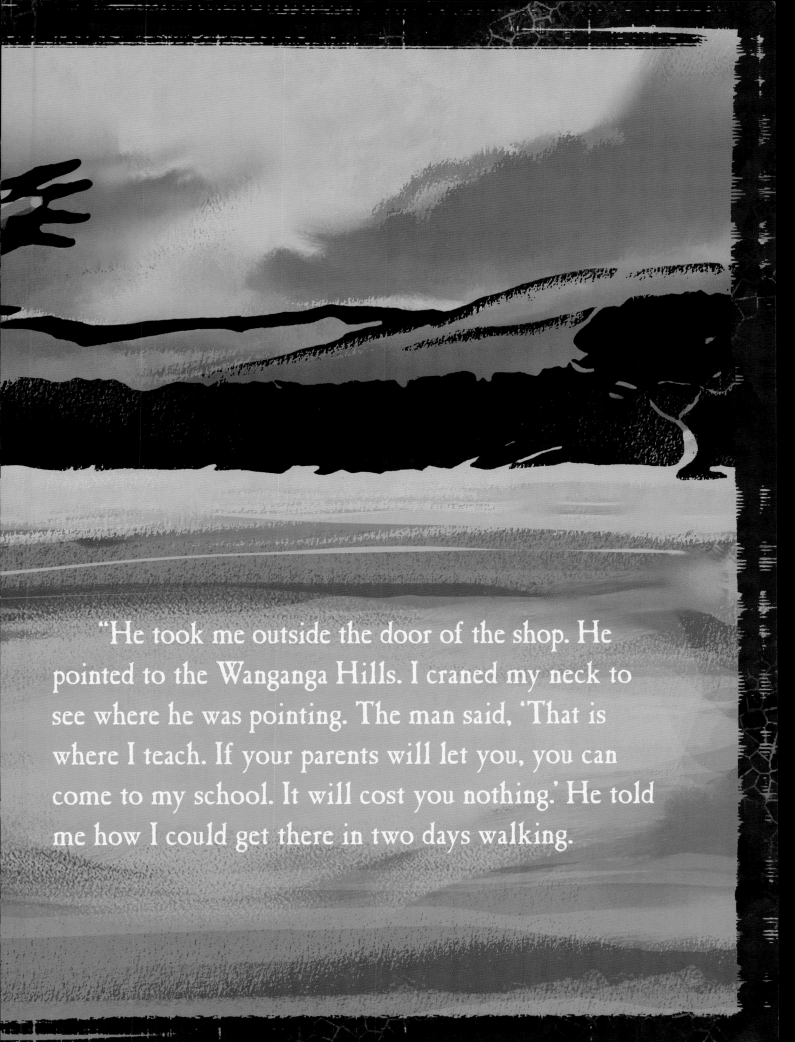

"He took me outside the door of the shop. He pointed to the Wanganga Hills. I craned my neck to see where he was pointing. The man said, 'That is where I teach. If your parents will let you, you can come to my school. It will cost you nothing.' He told me how I could get there in two days walking.

"I rode home and told my mother what the principal had said. The next day my mother went with me to the village to talk to the principal. We looked everywhere for him but he had gone to the school.

"My mother asked me if I remembered how he had told me to get there. She asked me if I wanted to go. I told her I remembered all of his directions. I really wanted to go and learn more. I remembered Akinyi.

"My mother cried, but she packed me some things in a carton for me. My father was also sad, but he knew I had to go if I wanted a better future.

"I set out the next morning early because I had to get to the first village before night came. I had no watch, but I knew time by where the sun was and how the shadows fell on the ground. I had to sleep at the village so I wouldn't be outside at night with the animals.

"I was wearing shorts. I had no shoes. The carton was on my head. I had two rivers to cross and neither one had a bridge. The first one was easy. Then I walked to the Nyaidho. This river had flooded just one day before. Two people had drowned. I sat there on the steep bank afraid even to step in. I knew how to swim, but I might drop my carton and lose all my things. So I sat and I waited for courage to come. But instead, tears filled my eyes. Behind me was my home – my childhood, too. Ahead lay my dreams – and the man I would be.

"As I waited there, unable to move, some local people helped me to cross. They were helping some women who were coming from market with kids on their backs. All of us got across safely with the villagers' help.

"As I walked, I saw lots of beautiful birds, and the sky was blue like it always was. Monkeys were in the trees. I saw brown cows and goats. No one kept their cows or goats inside a fence. The animals would wander around all day and come home at night. Maybe they felt safe at home at night like we did. Maybe they had a granny who told them stories about the night.

"The principal had told me to stay in a village that had a fence around it for the first night. I found the village and the house where the people welcomed me in. They had very little food, so I told them I wasn't hungry. Instead I went to sleep on their floor.

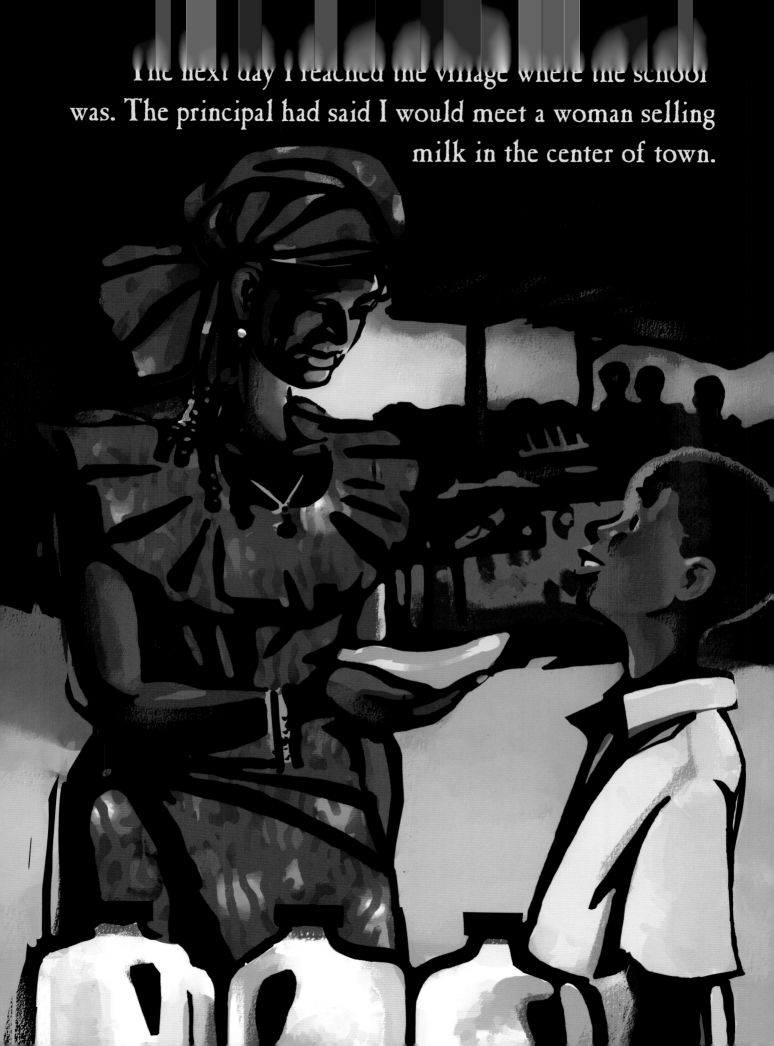

The next day I reached the village where the school was. The principal had said I would meet a woman selling milk in the center of town.

She would take me to the school. I found her, but she said I would have to wait until she finished selling her milk. She gave me a banana that tasted so good.

"She took me to the school where I would go to 7th and 8th grade. The principal was proud of me because I had showed him how important school was to me. I learned to love him very much. I was best at math, geography and soccer. I made good friends. I met my mother each Sunday at a church. It took her two hours to walk from our home to this church. I found a short cut to the church that only took me five hours. Other kids from my school had families at the church too, so they went with me. We always ran the whole way.

"I did well enough in that school to get sent to a Catholic boarding school for my high school years. Because I had good grades, I could attend for free. Even though I was far from my family and my village, they were happy for me because they knew I was beginning

to see my dream come true. There were 600 boys at the school, and I did well. The thing I remember most was that I got three meals every day. I was never hungry again.

"My teachers were from all over the world. One teacher was from Pennsylvania. I didn't know where Pennsylvania was. But I knew it was in the United States, which meant it was far away. He helped me a lot.

"There was also a doctor who helped me keep my
dream of becoming a doctor alive. I always remembered
how helpless I felt when my sister died.

"When I finished high school and was ready to go to college, I sent letters to colleges and universities around the world asking if they would accept me. Finally, a college in Texas said they would pay for me to attend there. But first I had to get money so I could travel to the United States.

"I showed that letter to my father and told him I wanted to go to Texas. He laughed at me. He had no money to send me so far away, so all he could do was laugh. But he did something that really surprised me. He was the only person in our village with a radio. People came from all over to listen to news on his radio. He loved that radio. He sold the radio to help me get money for my trip.

"I rode my bike everywhere, showing people the letter and asking them to help me get the money to go to Texas to become a doctor. People gave money to help me. I worked jobs to get money, too. In my village, there was a word that meant togetherness. That word was *"harrambee."* I will never forget how everyone helped me. I knew that someday I would help them.

"Finally, I raised enough money for the flight. When I was 17, I flew on a plane to the United States. Then I flew on another plane to Texas. Then I took a bus to Northwood College in Cedar Hills, Texas. I arrived with some clothes, a blanket and eleven dollars. That was all. But it was enough. I still have that blanket today.

"In Texas I continued my journey to become a doctor. I did well at the college. I studied hard. I also had time to play soccer. This time it was with a real ball!

"Then I was accepted into medical school. My dream was coming true!

"After three more years of school, I graduated and finally became what I promised my family and my village – a doctor!

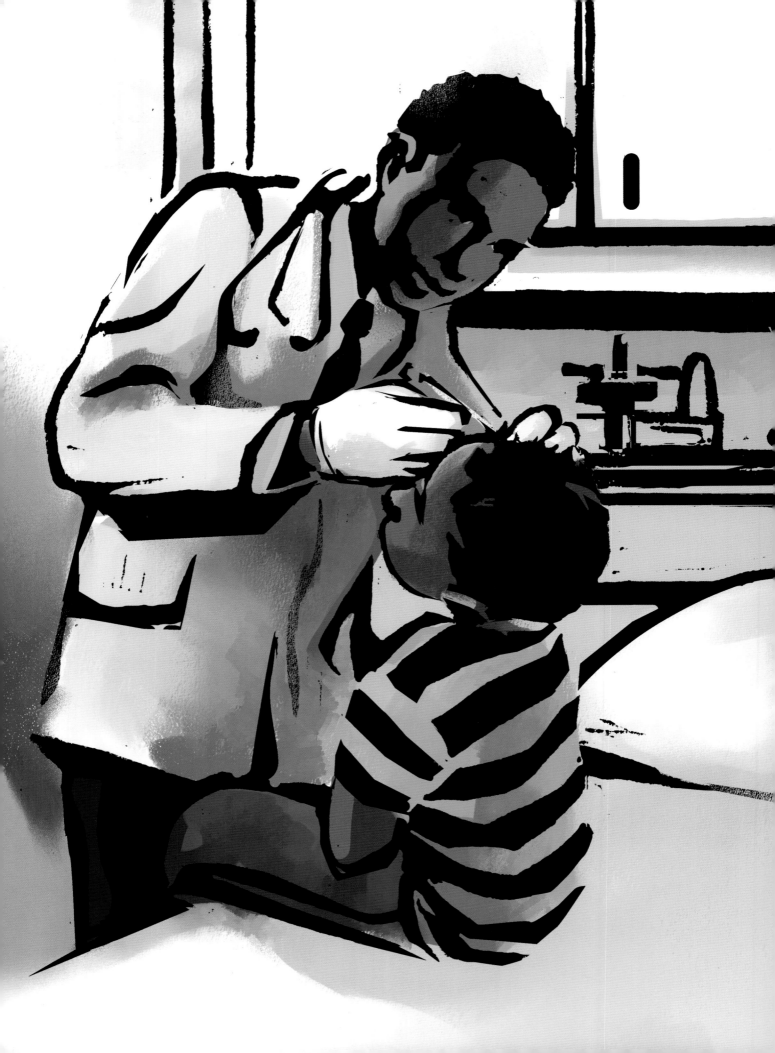

"A hospital in Akron, Ohio gave me the opportunity to continue my medical training. I worked hard and after a few years, with the help of many others, I had enough training to do what I had promised when I left my home more than 15 years before: build a clinic in my home village. It would have a nurse and medical supplies.

"I named it after my mother. She died while I was in medical training. On the clinic it says, 'Mama Pilista Bonyo Memorial Health Centre, Established, 2006.' I go back to the Clinic twice each year. I take young doctors and others to help me.

"We practice medicine. We also practice *harrambee* – togetherness.

"I would say to all children, follow your dream. Don't let anything stand in the way. Others will help you if they see you are determined. But if you need courage, look inside yourself - you will find it there."

The Author and Artists

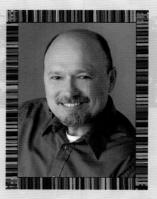

Vanita Oelschlager is a wife, mother, grandmother, philanthropist, former teacher, current caregiver, author and poet. A graduate of Mount Union College in Alliance, Ohio, she now serves as a Trustee of her alma mater and as Writer in Residence for the Literacy Program at The University of Akron. Vanita and her husband Jim were honored with a *Lifetime Achievement Award* from the National Multiple Sclerosis Society in 2006. She was the Congressional *Angels in Adoption* award recipient for the State of Ohio in 2007 and was named *National Volunteer of the Year* by the MS Society in 2008. Vanita was also honored in 2009 as the *Woman Philanthropist of the Year* by the Summit County Chapter of the United Way.

Kristin Blackwood is a teacher and frequent illustrator of books for children. Her works of art are published in: *My Grampy Can't Walk, Let Me Bee, What Pet Will I Get?, Made in China, Big Blue, Ivy in Bloom* and *Ivan's Great Fall.* A graduate of Kent State University, Kristin has a degree in Art History. When she isn't designing or teaching, she enjoys being a mother to her two daughters.

Mike Blanc is a life-long professional artist. His work has illuminated countless publications for both corporate and public interests worldwide. Accomplished in traditional drawing and painting techniques, he now works almost exclusively in digital medium. His first book, *Francesca*, was written by Vanita Oelschlager and published in autumn 2008. Their second collaboration, *Postcards from a War*, was released in 2009.

Bonyo's Kenya Mission

Dr. Bonyo with his journey blanket

All net profits from *Bonyo Bonyo* will go to Bonyo's Kenya Mission (bonyoskenyamission.org). This program was started by Dr. Bonyo when he was a medical student, and he was joined in 1997 by his teacher Dr. Daniel Marazon. Together, they raised funds, oversaw the development of programs and also the delivery of services for people living in and around Dr. Bonyo's childhood home in western Kenya.

Medical and educational services are provided through the Mama Pilista Bonyo Memorial Health Centre in the lovely village of Masara. The Centre is named after Dr. Bonyo's mother.

Bonyo's Kenya Mission provides resources for medical care, staff, and HIV/AIDS education and counseling, as well as funds to complete and maintain the Health Centre.

In addition, funds raised assist in providing children and teachers in the Masara Primary School with necessary uniforms, books and supplies.

Bonyo's Kenya Mission Inc. is a 501(c) (3) nonprofit organization. It is headquartered in Akron, Ohio, where Dr. Bonyo maintains his family medical practice.

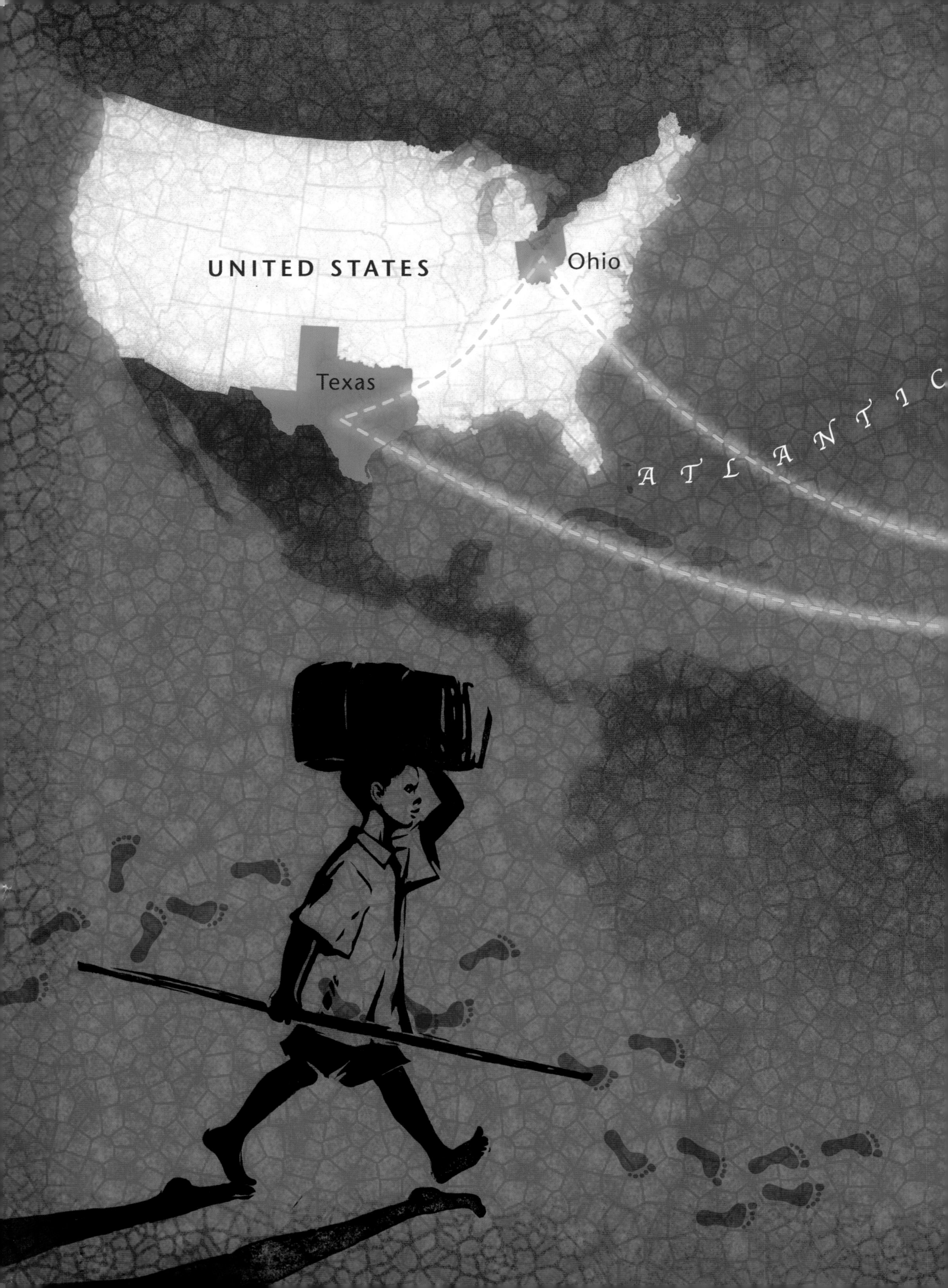
UNITED STATES
Ohio
Texas
ATLANTIC

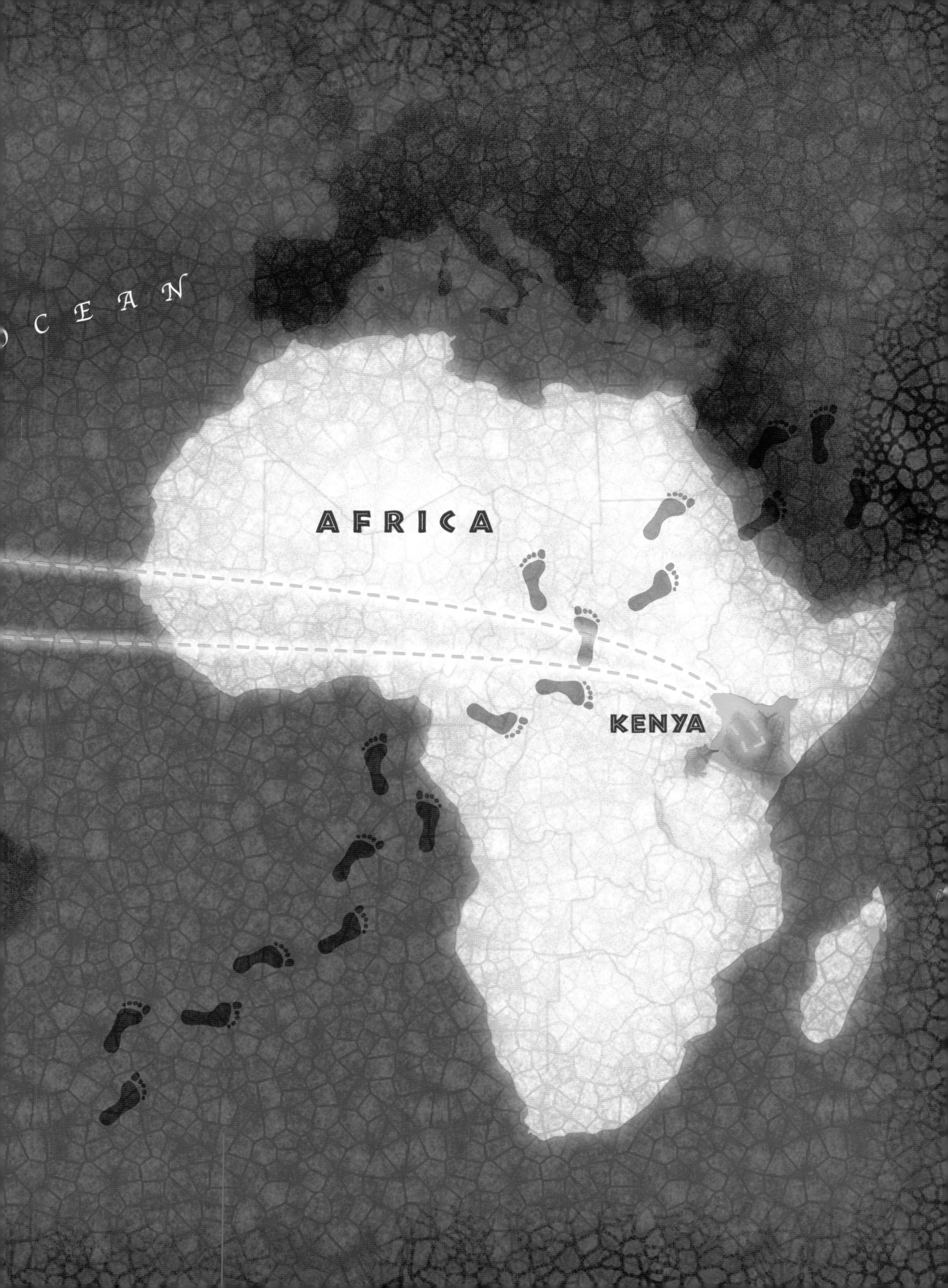
OCEAN
AFRICA
KENYA